B·I·B·L·E W·O·R·L·D

WORK AND SOCIETY
Everyday Life in Bible Times

Text by Margaret Embry

Published by
Lion Publishing plc
Sandy Lane West, Oxford, England
ISBN 0 7459 2179 5
Albatross Books Pty Ltd
PO Box 320, Sutherland, NSW 2232, Australia
ISBN 0 7324 0549 1

First edition 1994

Contributors to this volume
Margaret Embry is Tutor in New Testament Studies at Trinity
College, Bristol. She is also a contributor to *The Lion Encyclopedia
of the Bible*.

Alan Millard, Rankin Professor of Hebrew and Ancient Semitic
Languages at Liverpool University, is the consultant for the
illustrations in this book, and all the books in the series.

Acknowledgments
All photographs are copyright © Lion Publishing, except the
following:
British Museum: 8 (above left)
Alan Millard: 15 (below left)
Oxford Scientific Films/John Downer: 5 (below left)
Estate of Yigael Yadin: 20 (below near right)

The following Lion Publishing photographs appear by courtesy of:
the Biblical Resources Pilgrim Center, Tantur: 18 (above right)
the trustees of the British Museum: 3 (above right), 6 (middle
right), 7 (below left), 13 (below left), 14 (above right),
19 (below right)
the Eretz Israel Museum, Tel Aviv: 16 (below left and above right),
19 (below left), 20 (below far right)
the Haifa Music Museum: 3 (middle right, below right)
the Holy Land Hotel, Jerusalem: 4 (middle right)
the Rockefeller Museum: 7 (below left)

Illustrations, copyright © Lion Publishing, by:
Chris Molan: 1, 2 (left), 3, 4, 5, 6, 7, 8, 9, 10, 11, 12, 13, 14, 15, 16,
17, 18, 19, 20
Jeffrey Burn: 2 (right), 4 (above right), 5 (below right), 7 (far right),
9 (above right, middle right), 10 (far right), 16 (below right),
17 (below left), 18 (far right), 19 (middle left), 20 (above right)

Bible quotations are taken from the Good News Bible, copyright ©
American Bible Socitey, New York, 1966, 1971 and 4th edition
1976, published by the Bible Societies/HarperCollins, with
permission.

A catalogue record for this book is available
from the British Library

Printed and bound in Malaysia

BIBLE WORLD

WORK AND SOCIETY

EVERYDAY LIFE IN BIBLE TIMES

Margaret Embry

A LION BOOK

Contents

page 1

page 15

page 19

page 20

page 8

page 6

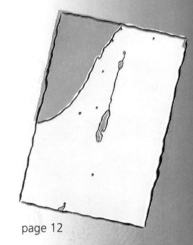

1 2,000 Years of Change

Over 2,000 years of history are described in the Bible. In that time, the way the nations were ruled changed a lot. Other things, such as the type of work done by craftworkers, stayed much the same.

These illustrations show the main stages in the history of the nations, which you can read more about in this book.

▲ 1 Nomads
Abraham and his family lived as nomads—travellers—in Canaan. Their flocks of sheep and goats provided milk and meat for food, as well as leather and wool for clothing and for the tents they lived in. They had to trade their goods with settled peoples for other things they needed, such as tools and weapons made of bronze. The head of the family was the leader of the whole family group.

▼ 3 A new nation
By the time Abraham's descendants escaped from Egypt they were a nation—the Israelites. God gave them laws, which were to guide them as they set up a new society for themselves, in which all nations would see God's standards at work.

◀ 2 Slaves
Abraham's descendants went to live in Egypt. They eventually became slaves, making bricks for the great building projects of the king of Egypt. They still thought of themselves as belonging to family groups named after sons of Jacob (Israel), who had come to Egypt in the first place.

5 Subjects of the king

Eventually the Israelites decided to have a king like other nations. This brought many changes. New types of job were created: some people were needed to serve in the full-time army; others were busy with the work of government, making sure the king's orders were carried out. There was more buying and selling of goods.

4 Settlers

The Israelites gradually made a home for themselves in Canaan. They were ruled not by a king but by God's laws. People lived together in small cities and farmed the land around. Each family made most of what it needed, but some people could now specialize in different kinds of work—such as making pots, or working metal. However, they had to trade with other nations for the latest in technology—especially the new and better iron tools and weapons that people had learned to make.

6 Ruled by emperors

Years later, the nation was defeated by enemies. Their way of life was influenced in turn by the strong nations who conquered them and made them part of their empires.

7 Roman rule

The Romans ruled the land in the time of Jesus. However, they let the people follow their own religion, and the religious teachers were widely respected.

2 Life and Worship

The Israelites really began to think of themselves as a nation when they escaped from slavery in Egypt. They believed that God had rescued them from their suffering: God was their real leader, who loved them and wanted the best for them.

During the long journey to the land of Canaan where they could make their home, God gave them laws about how to live and how to worship. Things would go well for their nation, they believed, if they lived by God's laws.

> *Hear, O Israel:*
> *the Lord your God is one God.*
> *Love the Lord your God with all your heart and with all your soul and with all your strength.*
>
> *Do not bear a grudge against someone else; instead, settle your quarrel, forget about taking revenge, and lay aside your hatred.*
> *Love your neighbour as you love yourself.*

Laws for a good life

God's laws were very detailed, giving instructions for all the different questions and concerns that people have to deal with in life: laws about how and where to worship, when to work and when to rest, how the wealthy should use their riches, how to look after the poor people in society, how people should behave in time of war... and many more things besides. In all the laws, it is clear that God is on the side of justice, loyalty, and love.

▼ The tabernacle

An altar and a huge basin of water stood in the tabernacle enclosure. Here the priests directed the people as they brought special offerings to God.

Only the priests could go inside the tent. In the first part stood a lampstand, an altar where incense was burned, and a table where bread was laid out.

A curtain screened the far end of the tent. In this innermost part was a special box called the ark of the covenant, or covenant box. It contained the stone tablets on which the ten great laws, the Ten Commandments, were written. Only the high priest was allowed in, and then only once a year, on the Day of Atonement.

A place to worship God

God's laws gave details about how the people should worship God. As they journeyed from Egypt to Canaan, they were given instructions about a special worship tent, called the tabernacle.

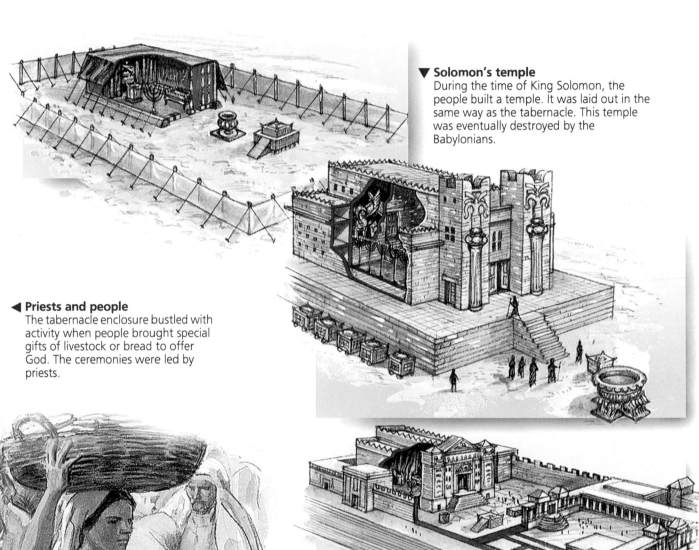

▼ Solomon's temple

During the time of King Solomon, the people built a temple. It was laid out in the same way as the tabernacle. This temple was eventually destroyed by the Babylonians.

◄ Priests and people

The tabernacle enclosure bustled with activity when people brought special gifts of livestock or bread to offer God. The ceremonies were led by priests.

▲ Herod's temple

Years later, when the people returned from exile in Babylon, they built a second temple. This was destroyed by the Romans, and in 19BCE King Herod the Great began work on a new temple. This was the temple that Jesus visited. It took 40 years to build.

3 Priests and Levites

God's laws said that some people should be chosen as priests who would lead the people by helping them to live as friends of God. They would teach people to understand all the laws, so that they could obey them. They were also in charge of the special ceremonies for worshipping God. These included sacrifices, in which the people offered to God a valuable part of their produce, such as animals from their flocks and grain from their harvest.

In some cases the produce was burned as part of the ceremony. In other cases, it was used by the priests after the ceremony, or eaten in a celebration meal by the worshippers.

A family of priests

All the priests had to be chosen from the tribe of Levi, one of the twelve original families in the nation of Israel. More than that, they had to be descended from Aaron, Moses' brother, who was a member of that tribe. The rest of the 'Levites' became assistants. A 'high priest' was appointed to be in charge.

There were still high priests, priests and Levites in New Testament times.

▼ **The high priest's clothing**
The high priest wore the same clothes as the ordinary priest, with ceremonial overgarments:

A blue headdress with a gold band with the words, 'Holy to the Lord'

The purse or breastpiece, with twelve precious stones to represent the twelve tribes of Israel

A special garment, the 'ephod', embroidered with gold, red, blue and purple

A blue robe edged with bells and pomegranates

Music for worship

One of the Levites' jobs was to provide music to worship God in the temple. They composed some of the Psalms —the hymns in the Bible— and organized colourful processions with singing, music and dancing. A trumpet was blown to call people to the tabernacle.

> *Praise God with the sounding of the trumpet,*
> *with the harp and lyre,*
> *with tambourine and dancing,*
> *with strings and flute,*
> *with the clash of cymbals.*
> *Let everything that has breath*
> *Praise God.*

▲ **A band of musicians**
The musicians in this military band from ancient Assyria are playing a hand-drum, five-string lyre, eight-string lyre and cymbals. Similar instruments were used by the Levites for temple music.

◄ **David's lyre**
This style of lyre is called a 'kinnor'. King David probably played a kinnor.

▼ **Lyre**
A woman plays a nine-string lyre in this ceremonial procession.

4 Judgment and Justice

If the people followed God's laws, they would be able to live in peace with their neighbours. Arguments happened when they didn't obey.

At the start, Moses settled disputes himself as he led the people from Egypt to their new land. When this job got too much for him—because the nation had grown so large—he appointed wise and experienced leaders to help. They were to be absolutely fair in making decisions. Justice was for everyone, whether they were foreigners or Israelites, rich or poor, powerful or weak.

When the Israelites settled in the land of Canaan, they appointed people in every town to make sure that quarrels were sorted out fairly.

The role of priests

The priests were experts in God's laws, so they were called in to help the judges in difficult cases. The people had to accept the priests' decision.

This is the reminder that God gave to Israel's judges:

Judge the people fairly.
Treat everyone in the same way.
Don't accept bribes ...
follow justice, and justice alone.

Putting things right

If someone was found to have done wrong to another, God's laws said that the damage should be made good. Sometimes this meant replacing what had been taken or destroyed. In other cases, the offender had to pay money as compensation.

The king's court

Long after the time of Moses and the giving of the law, Israel had its first kings. People could appeal to the king to help them settle quarrels. King Solomon was famous for his wise decisions.

Once, two women came to Solomon, arguing bitterly. Each of them had had a baby, but one baby had died. Now they both claimed to be the mother of the one that was still alive.

Solomon ordered the baby to be cut in half so that each could have a share. One of the women said no: she would rather the child were given alive to the other. Then Solomon knew she was the real mother, and gave her the child.

▶ **Solomon's justice**
Solomon judges a difficult case.

Punishment

Whipping was a common form of punishment. God's laws said there should be no more than forty strokes. Other nations could be much more severe in the way they treated criminals.

In Old Testament times the worst crimes received the death penalty. This was generally carried out by stoning. A crowd would gather round the condemned person and throw large rocks at them.

In New Testament times, the Romans did not allow the Jews to carry out the death penalty. Jesus' execution had to be approved by the Roman governor, Pilate, and he died by the Roman method of execution—being nailed to a cross of wood.

Prison

Only quite wealthy societies can afford to keep people in prison. In the time of Israel's kings, a prophet named Jeremiah was imprisoned by being thrown into an old water cistern. Other prisoners were kept in guardrooms in the palace.

In New Testament times, both King Herod the Great and the Romans built fortresses where people could be kept in prison.

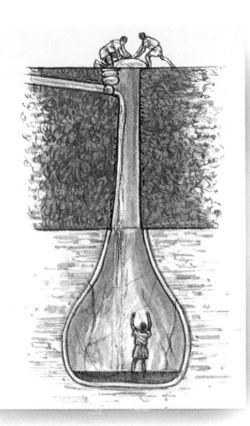

▶ **A dark, damp prison**
A disused water cistern made a dark, damp prison for the prophet Jeremiah.

▲ **Fort of Antonia**
The Fort of Antonia in Jerusalem was the garrison for the Roman soldiers. Paul was kept under guard for a while here.

Did you know?

By the time of Jesus, the Jews had a special council called the Sanhedrin. Part of the Sanhedrin's job at this time in their history was to help govern the people on behalf of the Romans, who had conquered their land. Another part was to deal with the most difficult cases of lawbreaking.

In Jesus' day, the person in charge of the council was the high priest. Jesus was brought before the Sanhedrin, accused of dishonouring God.

5 The Poor and the Sick

One thing that was special about God's laws was that they protected the weakest people in society.

The laws reminded people that, just as God had rescued the Israelites from slavery, they in turn should help the downtrodden.

▼ **Beggars**
Beggars were always to be seen. They would wait by the city gate for people to give them what they needed. Old people without families and people who could not work because of illness or disability would have to beg for a living.

Slaves

Slavery was widespread throughout Bible times. Prisoners of war were sold as slaves. Poor people who got into debt sometimes had to sell themselves or someone in their family into slavery. Slaves belonged completely to their masters.

God's laws said that slaves were to enjoy the weekly day of rest along with all the household. Israelite slaves were to be set free after six years, and given generous supplies of food and drink to give them a good start when they were free again.

Poor people

In Bible times, widows and their children were very likely to be poor. God's laws said that wealthier people should take care of them. At harvest time they must leave any of the crop that they dropped together with the crop around the edges of the field for the poor to gather. The people were to bring a tithe—a tenth of their produce—to the priests, and part of that was to be used to help the poor.

Foreigners

When the Israelites settled in a land of their own, they were enthusiastic about following God's laws. These laws treated people fairly, so it was no surprise that many people from other nations were keen to join them. The laws clearly said that they should be allowed to.

▶ **Spreading disease**
Rats and other vermin spread disease easily, fouling even the places where people lived.

Dealing with sickness

In ancient times there were many sick people. The water was dirty, there were no organized rubbish collections, rats brought plagues and flies spread disease. Many people had a poor diet, and this made them more likely to get sick. Babies might be born sickly. Sand and dust caused blindness.

Many of the laws God gave the people would have helped prevent sickness:

▶ The people were not to eat pork. (In a hot country, there was a high risk of food poisoning from pork.)

▶ The people were to have a complete rest one day in seven.

▶ The priests had to isolate people suffering from infectious diseases and cleanse or burn everything that might be contaminated.

▶ **A doctor's equipment**
Medical instruments like these were used by doctors around the time of Jesus. One of Jesus' followers was a doctor. His name was Luke, and in the book he wrote about Jesus' life, he shows special interest in the people Jesus healed.

Doctors

For most of Old Testament times there were no real doctors, but people used a range of home-made treatments: for example, mashed figs could be heated to make a poultice, which would draw out a boil, and soothing olive oil was put on wounds and sores.

By New Testament times, things had changed. Every town was required to have a doctor, and a surgeon too, if possible.

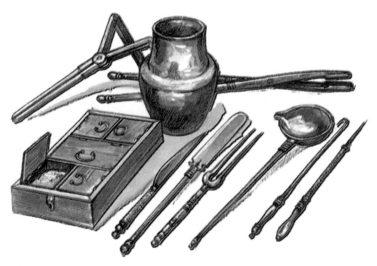

6 Kings

The Israelites never found it easy to live as God wanted, even when they had a land of their own. Sometimes they gave up trying. When that happened they grew weak, and enemies from the lands around preyed on them, taking land and livestock. When they asked God to help, God gave them leaders—called 'judges'—who led them to victory against their enemies. Gideon and Samson were both this kind of leader.

The last of the 'judges' was Samuel. He advised the whole nation about how to live as God wanted. In his day, however, the nation came under fierce attack from its enemies, and the people asked for a king, like the other nations. They believed that a strong leader would enable them to beat their enemies.

The first kings

When the nation demanded a king, Samuel warned them that this was not what God really wanted for them. Still they insisted. So Samuel, guided by God, chose the first king, Saul. Next came David, and then Solomon.

But Samuel had been right. The people found that their kings, like those of other nations, took away some of their freedom. They had to pay heavy taxes, work on special building projects for the king, and see him enjoying luxury at their expense.

Two kingdoms

After Solomon there was rebellion and the nation split into two kingdoms: Israel in the north, Judah in the south.

Israel had very few good kings, and the people forgot to live as God wanted. Around 700BCE Israel fell to the Assyrians, and the people were scattered.

In Judah, some of the kings did try to make sure the nation obeyed God. Others were selfish and cruel.

A hundred years after the kingdom of Israel was wiped out, the kingdom of Judah was defeated by the Babylonians, and the people were forced to go to far-off Babylonia.

From that point on, the Israelites, or Jews, were ruled by foreigners: after the Babylonians, the Persians took control. They let those who had been exiled go home if they wanted, and sent the Jews home. The Greeks took over from the Persians. Then, for a while, there were Jewish kings again—until the Romans took control.

▼ **Ivory carvings**
In the time of the two kingdoms, ivory carvings were much prized by the wealthy as decorations for their mansions and fine wooden furniture. One prophet, Amos, criticized the rich for buying luxuries while poor people went hungry. This is an ivory carving of a sphinx.

Jewish kings

A family of Jewish kings came to power following a revolt led by the family of Judas Maccabeus in 168BCE. At the time, foreigners ruled the land, and they were forcing the Jews to follow a different religion. The family of Judas Maccabeus marched into Jerusalem and restored the worship of God.

These fighters won a freedom that lasted about a hundred years. However, different family members constantly plotted against each other to become king. Meanwhile, the Romans grew more powerful: Herod the Great, who ruled when Jesus was born, was only in power because he had agreed to take orders from Rome.

7 Government Officials

Having a king brought many changes to Israel. In order to be strong leaders, the kings needed people to help make sure that everyone in the nation did what they said—officials who would help with government.

Working for the government

From the time of David and Solomon there were government stewards and secretaries. They kept state records and organized both the newly-created army and the teams of workers who were recruited to work on special building projects for the king. They looked after the collecting of taxes—often oil and wine rather than money—from the various areas of Israel.

Later on, when the Israelites were conquered by other nations, some of them had important jobs working for the foreign governments that ruled them.

◀ **A steward's seal**
Stewards sealed a scroll with a lump of wet clay, which they then stamped with their seal to show it was really from them. This seal is inscribed: '(belonging) to Shema, Servant of Jeroboam'. It dates from the time of Jeroboam II of Israel.

Household stewards

A steward was someone who worked for a wealthy household. A steward might organize what the servants did, and supervise what was spent. Abraham had a steward even when he lived as a nomad. This trusted steward was given the job of arranging his son's marriage. Joseph became a steward in the household of a wealthy Egyptian named Potiphar.

▶ **Scribes at work**
This Assyrian carving shows government scribes at work. It dates from around the time the northern kingdom of Israel fell to Assyria.

Scribes

The word 'scribe' simply means someone who writes things down. During the time of the kings, the word was used to mean a government secretary who kept the nation's records.

Public scribes

Public scribes hired out their services at the city gate to anyone who needed them—writing letters, making records of business deals, and so on.

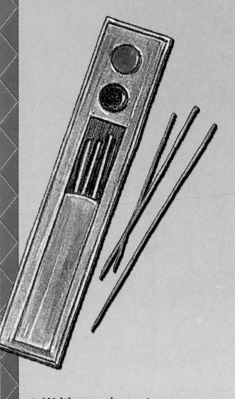

▲ **Writing equipment**
Rush pens are kept alongside blocks of red and black ink, in a scribe's pencil case dating from later Old Testament times.

Did you know?

In the time of Jesus the word 'scribe' was kept for scholars who studied God's laws and taught the people what they meant.

8 The King's Army

Saul, the first king of Israel, set up a permanent army in Israel. Until that point, the people had relied on volunteers banding together in time of need to fight their battles.

Centuries before, in the time of Abraham, nomadic family groups sometimes had to fight to protect themselves. Later, when the Israelites entered Canaan, Joshua organized the men of the nation into a fighting force until the job was done. Throughout the time of the 'judges', leaders got together armies when they were needed.

The permanent army

David, the king who followed Saul, really built up the army. He appointed a commander-in-chief and had a special bodyguard of thirty men.

There was a permanent army of six hundred men and a force of paid foreign soldiers. David also divided the land into twelve parts, and each division did military service for one month of the year. David's organization set the

▲ Ancient weapons
Spearheads found in the remains of Lachish—a city where the people of Judah fought first the Assyrians and later the Babylonians.

▼ Chariots
Solomon was the first Israelite king to set up a chariot force. He imported horses from Cilicia in the north and chariots from Egypt to the south. Chariots were light, made of wood, wicker and rope.

The Israelite chariot carried three fighting men, one of whom held a shield to protect the others. They usually had bows and arrows, with a quiver fitted to the chariot. They might also have throwing-spears. Chariots were often driven full speed at the enemy, to scatter them.

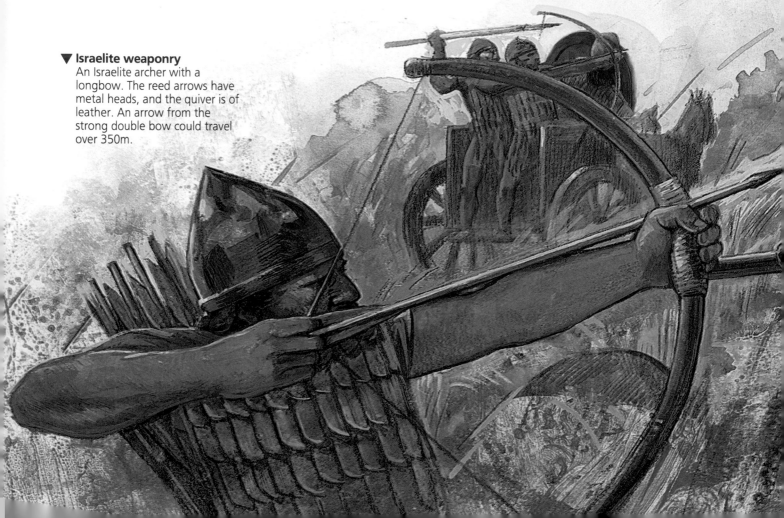

▼ Israelite weaponry
An Israelite archer with a longbow. The reed arrows have metal heads, and the quiver is of leather. An arrow from the strong double bow could travel over 350m.

style for a long time to come. After the kingdom split in two, King Ahab built up a powerful Israelite army, which beat the Syrian army in fierce battles .

The King's armies were disbanded after the defeat of the two kingdoms by the Assyrians and Babylonians.

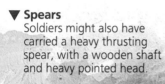

Did you know?

Freedom fighters led by the family of Judas Maccabeus were the nation's last successful soldiers. They used guerilla tactics to get rid of the people who ruled in the Greek Empire which Alexander the Great had established, and set up their own king and their own army.

▼ Armour

Armour was expensive, but a coat of leather gave some protection to the common soldier. Soldiers also carried shields. These were usually made of wood and covered with leather. Some shields had metal studs. Helmets might be of leather or metal.

Some soliders had scale armour —overlapping plates of metal sewn on to a coat of cloth or leather.

▼ Spears

Soldiers might also have carried a heavy thrusting spear, with a wooden shaft and heavy pointed head.

◄ Swords

The sword is the weapon most often mentioned in the Bible. In early times, swords were short, rather like daggers. By the time of the kings, soldiers were using long, straight iron swords.

9 On the Defensive

Throughout Bible times, most cities were built as fortresses. Strong walls protected people from their enemies. Soldiers could shower missiles on attackers from the height of the city wall and its towers.

The Israelites themselves had to attack the walled cities of the Canaanites when they settled Canaan. Once they had captured them, they repaired the fortifications for their own protection.

Solomon built forts at Megiddo, Hazor and Gezer. The fortifications at Megiddo were enlarged by another king, Ahab.

Herod the Great built a number of forts, with comfortable living quarters as well as rooms for soldiers and supplies.

Remains of some of these buildings still exist.

Enemy attack

The simplest way to take a city was to get the inhabitants to agree to surrender. This did happen. At the city of Shechem, archaeologists believe that the people were happy to make peace with Joshua and the Israelites. There is no sign of a battle.

If agreement could not be reached, the attackers would try to break through the walls. They might use battering-rams to force a gap, or dig around the base so that the walls would collapse.

In some cases, the attackers built earth ramps so that they could scale the walls.

▶ **Siege!**
In this scene Israelites hurl missiles including burning torches from the city wall on to attacking Assyrian soldiers. The Assyrians are using battering-rams to break down the city gate, while archers behind thick straw shields shoot at the defenders on the walls.

▲ **Ruined walls of Megiddo**
The ruins of Solomon's fort at Megiddo can still be seen. Here are dilapidated casemate walls with rubble infill.

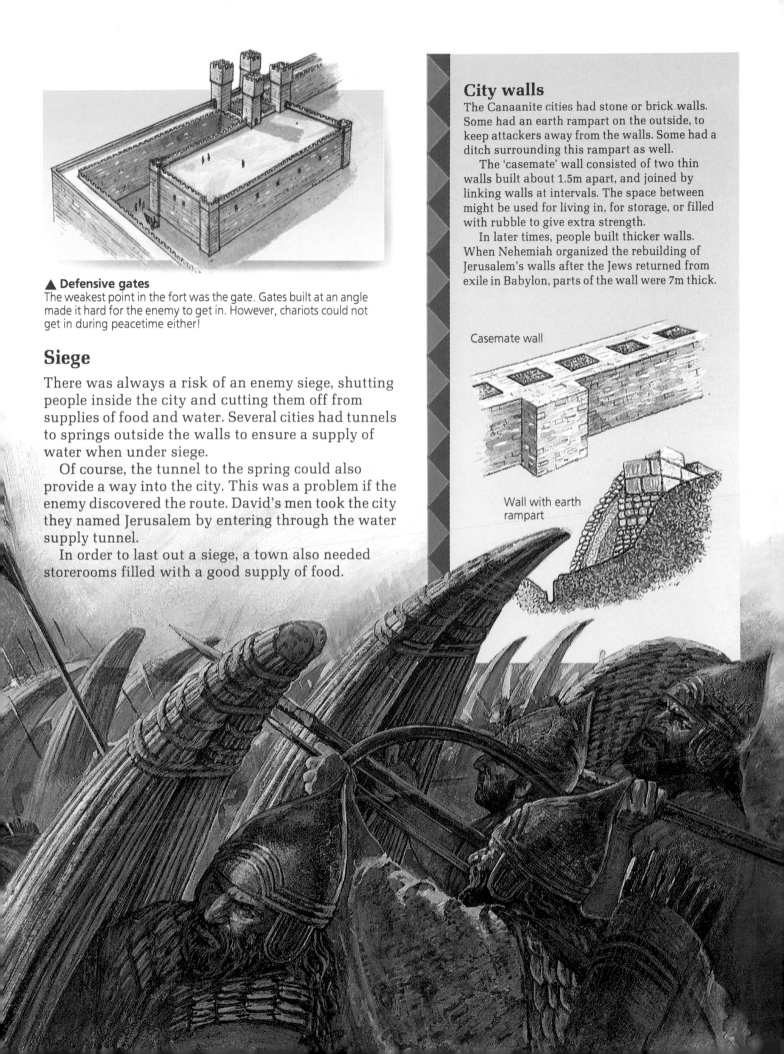

▲ Defensive gates
The weakest point in the fort was the gate. Gates built at an angle made it hard for the enemy to get in. However, chariots could not get in during peacetime either!

Siege

There was always a risk of an enemy siege, shutting people inside the city and cutting them off from supplies of food and water. Several cities had tunnels to springs outside the walls to ensure a supply of water when under siege.

Of course, the tunnel to the spring could also provide a way into the city. This was a problem if the enemy discovered the route. David's men took the city they named Jerusalem by entering through the water supply tunnel.

In order to last out a siege, a town also needed storerooms filled with a good supply of food.

City walls

The Canaanite cities had stone or brick walls. Some had an earth rampart on the outside, to keep attackers away from the walls. Some had a ditch surrounding this rampart as well.

The 'casemate' wall consisted of two thin walls built about 1.5m apart, and joined by linking walls at intervals. The space between might be used for living in, for storage, or filled with rubble to give extra strength.

In later times, people built thicker walls. When Nehemiah organized the rebuilding of Jerusalem's walls after the Jews returned from exile in Babylon, parts of the wall were 7m thick.

Casemate wall

Wall with earth rampart

10 Prophets

The Israelites' decision to have a king took them one step away from God's plan for their society. From the time of the kings they drifted further away from God's standards. Then God sent messengers—prophets—to remind them how to live.

These prophets spoke their message boldly. Sometimes they spoke to the people in the market-place; at other times prophets spoke to the nation's leaders—the king, or the priests.

Being a prophet was not a paid job! Nor was it welcome. Jeremiah and other prophets were very badly treated by the nation's leaders for being so outspoken.

Warnings

While the people lived in their own land, ruled by their own kings, there was still time to give warnings. Elijah and Elisha made it clear that the Israelites must be faithful to God—the one true God.

Later, prophets such as Amos, Hosea and Jeremiah told people to turn their lives around and follow God's standards ... or they could expect disaster. They were proved right when the nation was defeated by its enemies.

▼ **A warning rejected**
King Jehoiakim sneered at the advice of the prophet Jeremiah. As Yehudi read out the message, he cut off that bit of the scroll and threw it in the fire. But Jehoiakim's son suffered the defeat Jeremiah had warned him of.

Promises

The prophets also reminded the people of God's continuing love. When the people of Judah were defeated and taken to live in exile in Babylonia, prophets such as Ezekiel and Isaiah promised that God would act to help them.

Years afterwards, when the people returned home, other prophets encouraged them to remake their society according to God's standards. As a result they took the laws seriously again, and built a new temple where they could worship God.

Ezekiel said that the nation's leaders had been like bad shepherds who leave their sheep at the mercy of wolves while they laze around and enjoy themselves. God would act to help them, as a good shepherd takes care of sheep.

Isaiah spoke of the birth of a king: God's special king who would come one day to bring peace and justice.

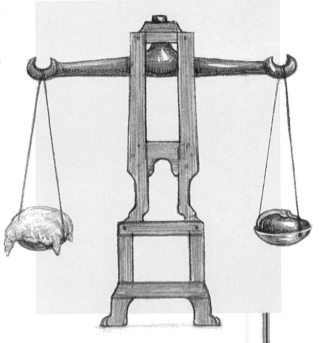

▲ Fairness
Amos reminded the people that God's standards were fair. Cheating people by using false scales was wrong.

True prophets
How can you tell a real prophet from someone who just fancies their own ideas? The Bible gives a clear answer: what a real prophet says comes true, and everyone can see it.

▶ Right standards
A plumbline—a weight hanging from a cord—hangs perfectly vertical. Builders used such a tool to make sure the walls were straight.

The prophet Amos said God's standards for right living were like the true vertical that the builder sees in the plumbline.

The First Synagogues

After the defeat of Israel and Judah, those who were left of the Israelite nation were ruled by foreign kings and emperors. They faced special problems about how to survive foreign rule without letting go of their loyalty to God.

Exile

The people of Judah who were forced into exile in Babylon had to set up new communities. They were to a large extent free to do as they wanted. They were allowed to build their own homes in special areas set aside for them in the capital itself and in other towns. They were free to earn their own living. They were even permitted to keep their own customs and religion.

God's laws in a foreign land

However, the destruction of the temple in Jerusalem by the Babylonian army meant it was no longer possible to have religious ceremonies in the way the law described them.

Instead, people made even more of those parts of the law they could still keep—things like keeping the seventh day, the sabbath, as a day of rest, and following the details of the food laws. The written records of what God had said to their people became very important, and some of the priests made a careful study of them. Many of the books that today form the Old Testament were written out in their final form when the nation was in exile.

▼ **In the synagogue**
The inside of a synagogue as it may have looked during a sabbath meeting in the time of Jesus. The women and children sit on one side, the men on the other, with prayer-shawls covering their heads.

The ruler of the synagogue kept order and invited people to read and speak.

The assistant gave out the scrolls. He may also have blown a trumpet from the roof at sunset on a Friday evening, a sign that the sabbath had begun, and work must stop.

Men would stand on a wooden platform to read from the Bible.

Synagogues

Local meeting places, called synagogues, were set up in every Jewish community. When the Persians took control of the region, the Jews learned to speak the international language, Aramaic, and not Hebrew. But the Bible was written in Hebrew, so children had to go to the synagogue school to learn the language. On the sabbath, everyone went to hear the Bible read aloud and to have it explained.

Teaching in the synagogue

The people who taught in the synagogue were the scribes: they were experts in God's law, and also knew all the teachings and rules of scholars through the ages. This was called the 'oral law' or 'tradition of the elders'. They also taught in the temple.

Scribes were highly respected, and when people spoke to them, they called them 'Rabbi'.

◀ Synagogue furniture
Notice the cupboard where the scrolls of God's law were kept. In some synagogues, a chest of scrolls may have been brought in for the meeting from an adjoining room.

Seven-branched lampstands similar to the one made for the tabernacle were placed in many synagogues.

Around the side of the room stone steps served as benches.

▲ Symbols in stone
Symbols carved in stone decorate the ancient synagogue at Capernaum. This picture shows a pair of pomegranates. This synagogue stands on the foundations of an older one—perhaps the one that existed in Jesus' day.

Jews abroad

By the time of Jesus, there were groups of Jews living in many different countries in the Roman Empire, and they, too, had synagogues as meeting places. When the first Christians went out telling people about Jesus, they often had the opportunity to talk to Jews in these synagogues.

12 Travel by Land

Several important routes passed through the land of Israel. Throughout ancient times, Egypt was a powerful and important country to the south, and different empires rose and fell in the lands to the north. The routes were needed to provide a link between the two. In times of peace, they were used for trade. In times of war, armies would march through.

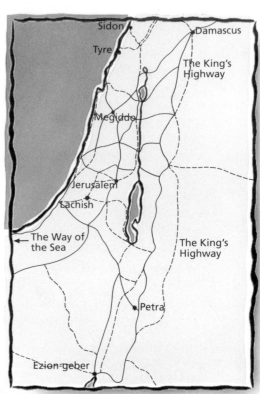

▼ Safety in numbers
Throughout Bible times people often chose to travel as part of a trading 'caravan'. Being part of a large group meant that they were less likely to be attacked by bandits.

▶ Routes
This map shows the main routes through the land of Israel in Old Testament times.

Old Testament times

In Old Testament times, the routes consisted of trodden tracks. They were suitable for travel on foot or by pack animal. Most travellers walked, but traders usually transported goods by 'caravan'- –long strings of pack animals. The ass was often used as a pack animal. In later times, the camel was used too, particularly by people from the desert regions.

Two- or four-wheeled wooden carts, often drawn by one or two oxen, were used throughout Bible times to transport goods and people. But they could only be used on flat ground and in the summer. When it rained the wheels got stuck in the mud.

Horses were used to pull chariots. Chariots could only make slow progress over rough roads. Except for their use in war, they were kept for ceremonial processions around the paved streets of cities.

▼ Carts
When the people of Judah were taken into exile they may have travelled in carts similar to this one.

New Testament times

By New Testament times, the Romans had taken control of the lands around the Mediterranean Sea, and they built paved roads with bridges and tunnels between the main cities throughout their empire. They built roads so that their armies could travel swiftly to where they were needed. But the same roads made travel easier for everyone—traders, people looking for work and people travelling to pay taxes or attend a religious festival.

Most people still travelled on foot or by donkey. However, horse-drawn carts and carriages could be used on the paved roads. Soldiers and messengers might travel by horse.

▶ Roman roads
Roman roads were made of several layers of packed stones and topped with paving. A Roman mile was 1000 paces— 1,478 metres.

13 Travel by Water

The Israelites were not a seagoing people. However, throughout Bible times, ships were important for trade and war.

On the Mediterranean

Many different types of ship were used on the Mediterranean Sea. Warships, eight or ten times as long as they were wide, had a double bank of oars so that they could move swiftly whatever the wind was like—although many had a sail as well.

Merchant ships were rounder, only three or four times as long as they were wide. They relied more on their sail, although most had oars that could be used when needed.

Many of these boats had two large steering oars at the stern.

Shipping routes

In early times the Phoenicians controlled most of the shipping routes. From their major ports at Byblos, Tyre and Sidon they built up a fleet of ships which travelled all round the Mediterranean.

King Solomon took charge of trade throughout Israel during his reign. He also developed his own fleet of merchant ships, and employed expert Phoenician sailors to run it.

River transport

River boats were often used for transport in ancient times. Both Egypt and Babylon, where the people of Israel lived at different times in their history, had navigable rivers. River boats do not have to stand up to huge waves so lightness is more important than strength. Some river boats were canoe-shaped, made from bundles of tightly-packed reeds. Others were coracles—round boats made of wicker and covered with tar or animal skins (or both) to make them waterproof.

▲ **Reed canoes**
In this painting from ancient Egypt people in reed canoes are hunting waterbirds in the shallow papyrus swamps of the River Nile.

▼ A Roman warship
Throughout Bible times most warships were equipped with oars, so they could travel at speed even when the wind was unfavourable.

Safe from pirates
The Romans ruled the lands around the Mediterranean in New Testament times. They brought peace to the region and trade could flourish. The Romans made sure that trade by sea was safe from pirates.

▼ Seagoing vessels
In the time of the kings, ships similar to these sailed the Mediterranean Sea. The Phoenicians were the great seafarers of the era.

14 Buying and Selling

In Bible times, buying and selling would normally take place at the market that was held just inside the town gates. People would display their wares simply—perhaps on a piece of woven cloth, in baskets or sacks on the ground, or on a simple stall.

Most of the sellers would be local people, taking this opportunity to meet as a community to buy and sell what they had produced on their own land or in their workshop. As today, craftworkers would also take special orders from customers, and make goods exactly to their requirements.

▼ **The market-place**
Buyers haggle over prices in this market-place scene from New Testament times.

Weights and measures

God's laws stated clearly that people should use fair weights and measures. People didn't always obey, and the Bible is full of reminders:

> *This is what God says: You have gone far enough, you princes of Israel. Give up your violence and oppression and do what is just and right... You are to use accurate scales and measures.*

▲ **Lion weights**
This set of lion weights, from ancient Assyria, is a good example of the sort of weights that would have been used in Bible times.

Business dealings

God's laws gave some strict rules about business dealings. They were often broken, but they show that God is on the side of fair dealing, honesty, and real care for others.

> *If someone leaves their cloak as a guarantee that they will come back and pay what they owe, you must let them have it back at sunset. It is all they have to sleep in!*
> *Don't take a person's millstones as a guarantee that they will pay their debts. They need them to make a living.*

▲ **A market in the Middle East**
Anyone visiting the Bedouin market at Beersheba today might think they had stepped back into Bible times.

15 Money

In the earliest Bible times, people bartered their wares: they exchanged one type of produce for another to get what they needed.

People's wealth was measured in terms of what they owned—their sheep, goats and cattle, and their gold and silver. In Abraham's day, these precious metals were often made into jewellery.

The barter system works well in small communities, and it would certainly have continued among neighbours throughout Bible times. However, it quickly becomes awkward to operate on a larger scale. It is easier to have some way of pricing things.

Gold, silver and copper

Over the years, it became usual to use precious metal to trade with. Silver was most commonly used, but copper and gold were used too. At first it was simply the weight of a particular metal that counted. Scales and measures were needed to weigh out the metal. When Abraham's wife, Sarah, died, he bought a cave for her tomb and paid a considerable weight of silver for it.

Coins

Around the seventh century BCE, coins were made. This made it easier to price goods and to trade them.

◀ **The emperor's image**
Many of the coins used in New Testament times bore the image of the Roman emperor—a constant reminder to the nation that they were under foreign rule.

▶ **Tax collectors**
In Roman times, tax collectors might work from a booth in the market-place.

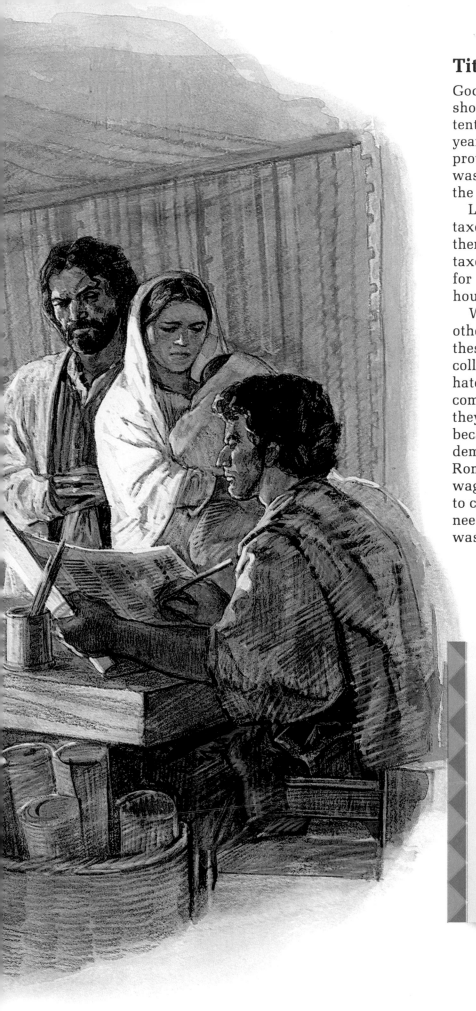

Tithes and taxes

God's laws said that the people should pay 'tithes': they should give a tenth of their produce to God each year. Some of this tithe was used to provide a living for the priests; the rest was used to help the poorer people in the community.

Later, the people also had to pay taxes to the king. Israel's kings made themselves unpopular by demanding taxes to pay for a full-time army and for a luxurious lifestyle for the royal household.

When Israel was conquered by other nations, they had to pay taxes to these nations. In Jesus' day, Jews who collected taxes for the Romans were hated by other people in the community. This was partly because they resented Roman rule, and partly because many of the tax collectors demanded more than was fair. The Romans did not pay the tax collectors wages: to make a living at all, they had to charge the people more than they needed to give to the Romans, and it was a great temptation to be greedy.

A prayer about riches

Give me neither poverty nor riches,
but only my share of food to eat.
Otherwise I may have too much and disown you, saying 'Who is God?'
Or I may become poor and steal, and so dishonour God.

16 The Potter

Once the Israelites had settled in the land and their farms produced good harvests, some people were able to spend more time working at other jobs. They could then trade what they made for the farm produce they needed.

Throughout Bible times, there were more potters than any other kind of craftworker. Clay pots broke easily, so there was always a steady demand.

▼ **Clay**
Red clay was left to be broken up by sun, rain and frost. Then, the right amount of water was poured on the clay. People trampled the water into the clay to make a thick, sticky mud.

Scrap pads
Pots often broke during firing. The pieces, called potsherds, were used for writing notes on—they were the scrap paper of Bible times!

▼ **Sun dried**
Pots are left to dry in the sun for several days before firing.

Kilns
The firing of the clay in a kiln was the ultimate test of a potter's art!

Workshops
Caves made good pottery workshops—cool in summer and warm and dry in winter. Pottery workshops, whether in caves or buildings, were usually grouped together, often just outside towns and cities, so that the smoke from the kilns was not a nuisance.

Storage jar
This large storage jar has a 'dipper' jug kept on a stick so that people can scoop out whatever is kept inside.

Shaping
Simple shapes could be pinched by hand.

A potter at work
A present-day potter shapes clay on the wheel in the traditional manner.

Potter's wheel
Mostly, the clay was shaped on a wheel. This one has a lower wheel, which the potter kicks to keep it turning.

Changing styles
In early Bible times, oil lamps were little more than a clay saucer with one side pinched into a lip to support the wick. By New Testament times lamps had spouts and were made in moulds. The upper half and lower half were then pressed together.

17 The Carpenter

It is quite easy to make things from wood, and in Bible times many families would have made their own simple furniture and tools, as well as shaping the wood they needed for building their homes. However, there were some specialist carpenters.

Did you know?

King Solomon built himself a palace that became known as the 'Palace of the Forest of Lebanon'. This was because its walls were panelled with beautiful cedarwood from the Lebanon, sent by King Hiram of Tyre.

◄ Cedar of Lebanon

Very fine cedar trees grew in the mountains of Lebanon. Cedar wood is dark and long-lasting, and has a very sweet scent.

▼ A carpenter's workshop

Part of the carpenter's work was to provide timber for house beams and lintels, so carpenters often did general building work as well. In the workshop, however, they might make smaller items such as yokes, ploughs, threshing-boards, carts, furniture, wheels, tools and boxes. The carpenter here is using a draw knife to shape the wood.

▼ Tools

Carpenters' tools have changed little over the centuries. These styles were common in New Testament times.

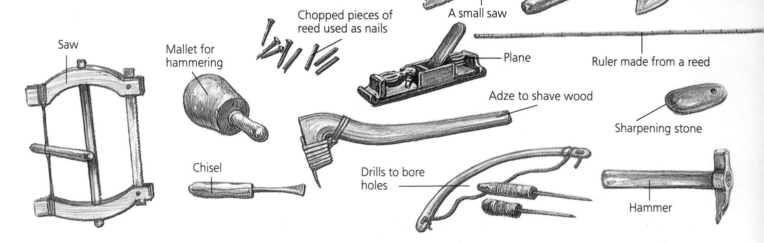

A small saw

Axe

Chopped pieces of reed used as nails

Saw

Mallet for hammering

Plane

Ruler made from a reed

Adze to shave wood

Sharpening stone

Chisel

Drills to bore holes

Hammer

The Builder

From the time the people of Israel settled in Canaan, just about everybody was a builder. When a family needed a home, the community would get together to help them build it, using local materials.

As time went by, some people became specialist builders. These more skilled workers were also needed to build more elaborate homes for the very wealthy, as well as palaces and other important buildings for kings.

▼ Working in the quarry

The local limestone was quarried for fine building. Holes were bored in the rock and wooden wedges driven in. These were soaked to make them expand, which split the rock. Then the workers could cut out large blocks with picks. They shaped these roughly and then transported them on sledges to the building sites. Skilled masons shaped the stones and fitted them into place, probably using pulleys and rollers. These carefully fitted stones needed no mortar to hold them together.

◄ The temple wall

Massive stones were used to build the temple at the order of Herod the Great.

Everyday buildings

Some places in Israel are very stony. In these areas people gathered stones from the fields and piled them up to make walls for their buildings. They filled any gaps with smaller stones.

In other places they made bricks out of mud and straw. Sometimes a mould was used to help shape them. The bricks were left to dry in the hot sun, which burned all summer long, or they were baked in a kiln. Then people laid a foundation of large stones, and built brick walls on top.

The roof was made from wooden beams laid across the walls. A layer of branches was placed on top, and the whole covered with a thick layer of mud.

Both brick and stone houses needed to be plastered inside and out to fill any gaps. Without this finish there would be many small openings which insects and snakes could get through. Mud was used as plaster; it was easily damaged by heavy rain, and needed a lot of maintenance.

Jesus the builder

When Jesus was a young man, there was a huge building project underway in Galilee, where he lived. The local ruler, Herod Antipas, decided to rebuild the ancient city of Sepphoris using Greek styles and plans. Tens of thousands of people worked on it. It is quite possible that Jesus would have worked as a carpenter and builder on the construction sites there.

▲ **Crane**
A reconstruction of the type of crane that Herod the Great's workers might have used to shift blocks of stone.

▼ **Builder's tools**
This collection of tools includes chisels, a mallet and a plumbline.

19 The Metalworker

In the ancient world, new discoveries in metalworking led to great advances in technology.

The first great breakthrough came when people discovered that by mixing two metals, copper and tin, they could make a metal that was harder than either of them. This was bronze, and it was hard enough to make tools and weapons that were sharper and stronger than the stone tools they had used before. This new era of technology was called the Bronze Age, and the Bible story of Abraham begins in that period.

Later, people discovered how to use iron, in what became known as the Iron Age. Iron is harder still, and makes better weapons. The first nations to master the technology of making iron had a big advantage in war. The Philistines, who were among Israel's main enemies during the time they were settling in the land of Canaan, had just this advantage. The Israelites had to go to the Philistines to get iron weapons and have them repaired! It was only after the time of Solomon that Israel had its own workshops for using iron.

In fact, the Israelites were never leaders in technology. As a result, other nations often had the advantage over them. Yet they were constantly reminded that real strength had nothing to do with technology—it lay in their relationship with God.

▼ **In the workshop**
Two workers pour molten metal into moulds to make tools. When the metal has cooled and hardened, another worker takes the tools out of the mould and polishes them smooth with a stone.

▲ **Furnace**
A side view through a furncace, showing the pots in which ore is melted.

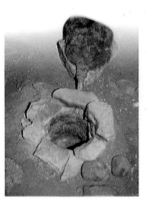

▶ **A smelting pit**
Sometimes ore was melted in a smelting pit. The black bellows were pumped by foot, to force air into the fire.

In the workshop

In ancient times, most metalworkers had small workshops, and they served the local area. They bought the metal they needed in lumps or bars from travelling merchants. The craftworkers melted the metals down in furnaces and shaped them in clay or stone moulds.

Only copper and iron were mined in Israel itself. Other metals were imported. Gold and silver came from Egypt and Arabia.

Gold and silver

Gold was probably the first metal to be used in ancient times, because it is easy to work. Silver is also easy to work, but it tarnishes, and was therefore less prized.

From earliest times gold and silver were used for jewellery and luxury items such as special cups, bowls and plates. Gold was often melted and beaten into sheets that could be used to cover wooden objects.

Treasure

Having lots of gold and silver treasure was the sign of being rich and successful in Bible times. But the Bible has several reminders that only people who live as friends of God, obeying God's laws, have something of lasting value. One of the Bible's hymns, Psalm 19, says this:

God's laws are right and true.
They are more precious than gold,
even lots of pure gold.

◄ Gold vessels
These gold vessels were discovered in Ur—the city where Abraham lived. They date back to centuries before the time of Abraham.

The Leatherworker

Leather is animal skin. In Bible times people used mainly sheep and goat skins. The person who made these into leather was called a tanner.

Tanners

The work of a tanner was very unpleasant. The first task was to cut the skins from the dead animals and wash them thoroughly, perhaps treating them with the juice of certain plants and removing the hair by soaking the skins in lime. Then the skins were hung out to dry. Sometimes they were dyed.

It was a smelly job! The tanner's workplace was always outside the town.

Did you know?

Many people looked down on tanners because of the work they did. The law given at the time of Moses said that anyone who touched dead bodies was 'unclean', and could not come into God's temple. Jesus said that the Jews had misunderstood laws like this: people could not be made 'unclean' in God's eyes by anything outside them. It was wrong thoughts inside, leading to wrong actions, that made them 'unclean'.

▼ **A smelly job**
Washing and drying skins to make leather was a smelly job, made rather more bearable if done out of doors.

▼ Leather goods

Craftworkers sewed the prepared leather into a variety of articles, such as tents, belts, purses, buckets and sandals. Helmets and shields were sometimes made of tough hide. An especially fine type of leather was prepared and sewn into long strips, to be used as scrolls.

The purse, bag, sandal and scroll below are based on discoveries from New Testament times.

New wine, new bottles

Leather bottles were made for carrying water, milk or wine. New wine needed a new wineskin, which had some 'stretch' in it, to make room for the gases caused by fermentation. A dry old wineskin would burst.

▼ Skin churn

A whole animal skin has been used to make this churn for milk. Churns like this would have been used in Bible times, and are still used by Bedouin who live in and around Israel today.

Phylacteries

The laws God gave said that the people should 'tie the law to their arms and head'—in other words, God's laws should govern what they thought and what they did. In Jesus' time—and still today—the Jews put short extracts from the Law into small leather boxes that they tie with thongs to their foreheads and left arm when they pray. These were called phylacteries (*tephillin* in Hebrew). They were a reminder to the wearer how important it was to keep God's laws.

A portable reminder

This phylactery from the time of Jesus is smaller and flatter than most modern phylacteries.

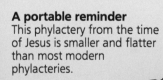

Finding Out More

If you want to know more about what you've read in *Work and Society*, you can look up the stories in the Bible.

The usual shorthand method has been used to refer to Bible passages. Each Bible book is split into chapters and verses. Take **1 Samuel 16:14–23**, for example. This refers to the first book of Samuel; chapter 16; verses 14–23.

When a reference to a Gospel story has other references after it in brackets, this means that the same story has been told by more than one of the Gospel writers.

1   2,000 Years of Change

Deuteronomy 26:5–9	**Nomads; slaves; a new nation; settlers**
1 Samuel 8:10–17	**Subjects of the king**
Matthew 8:5–13 (Luke 7:2–9)	
	A Roman centurion and Jesus

2   Life and Worship

The books of Deuteronomy and Leviticus	
Laws for a happy life	
Exodus 25:9—27:19	**A place to worship God**
Exodus 30:1–6, 17–18	**The tabernacle**

3   Priests and Levites

Exodus 28:1–3	**The first priests**
Luke 10:30–35	**A priest and a Levite**
Exodus 28:4–42	**The high priest's clothing**
1 Samuel 16:14–23	**David's lyre**

4   Judgment and Justice

Exodus 18:13–26	**Judging the people fairly**
1 Kings 3:16–28	**Solomon's judgment**
Deuteronomy 25:2–3; Joshua 7; John 18:28–32	
	Punishment
Jeremiah 38:1–6	**Jeremiah in prison**
Acts 21:30–36	**Paul in prison**
Matthew 26:57; Mark 14:53; Luke 22:66	
	The charge against Jesus

5   The Poor and the Sick

Exodus 22:21–27	**Slaves in Egypt**
Exodus 20:10	**A day of rest for slaves**
Exodus 21:2–6; Deuteronomy 15:12-14	
	Slaves set free
Ruth 2; Deuteronomy 14:22–29	
	Generosity to the poor
Numbers 15:15–16; Isaiah 56:6–7	
	Foreigners welcomed
Leviticus 11:7	**Food laws about pork**
Leviticus 13:1–46	**What to do about disease**
Isaiah 38:1–22	**Cure for King Hezekiah**

6   Kings

Judges 6:1—8:28	**Gideon**
Judges 13:1–16:30	**Samson**
1 Samuel 8:1–5	**The people want a king**
1 Samuel 8:10–1 Kings 11:43	
	The first kings
1 Kings 12:1–20	**Rebellion**
2 Kings 17:1–6	**The fall of Israel**
2 Kings 25:1–12	**The fall of Judah**
Ezra 1:1–4	**The return of the exiles**
Amos 5:11–12, 6:4	**Amos criticizes the rich**
1, 2 Maccabees	**Jewish revolt**

7   Government Officials

Daniel 1:1–6	**Working for the Babylonians**
Luke 16:1–9	**A dishonest steward**
Genesis 24:1–67	**Abraham's steward**
Genesis 39:1–6	**Joseph, Potiphar's steward**
Jeremiah 36	**Baruch, Jeremiah's scribe**
Matthew 9:1–8 (Mark 2:1–12; Luke 5:17–26)	
	Jesus and the scribes

8   The King's Army

Psalm 11:1–3; 2 Samuel 11:23–25	
	Enemy arrows
1 Samuel 18:6–11	**Saul's spear**
1 Samuel 17:32–40	**David refuses Saul's armour and sword**
1 Kings 10:26–29	**Solomon's chariots**
2 Samuel 23:18–39	**David's bodyguard**
1, 2 Maccabees	**Freedom fighters**

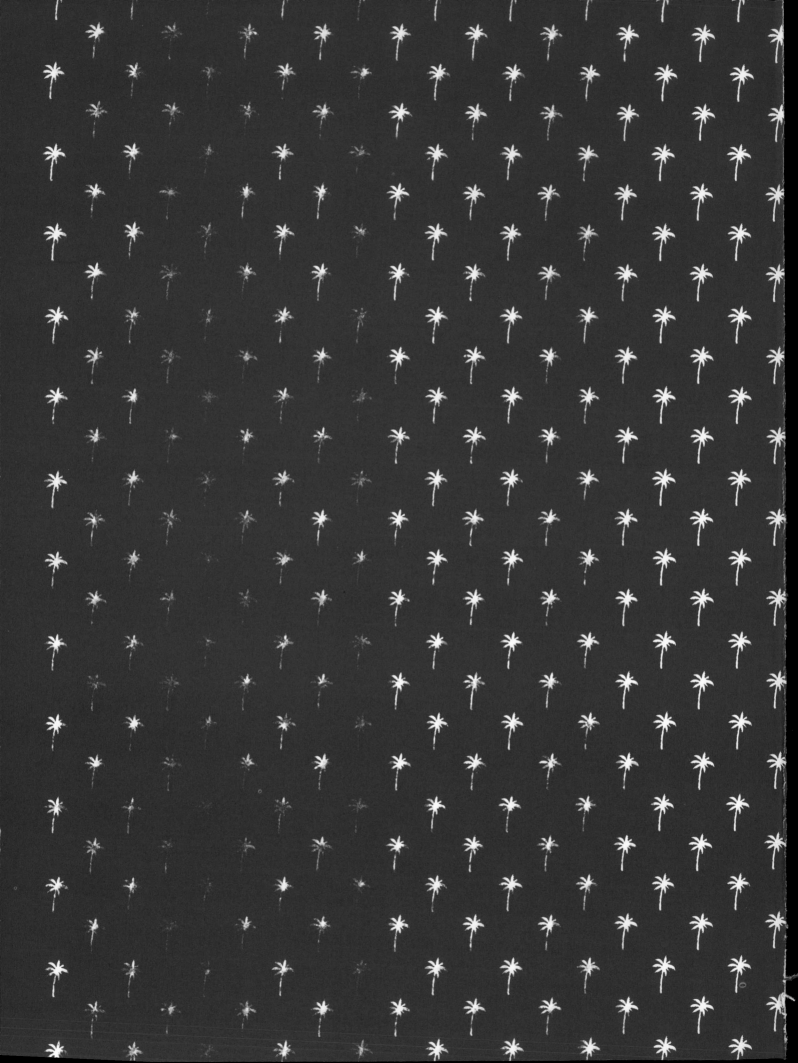